THE LITTLE BOOK OF
PATRICK MAHOMES

First published in 2025 by OH
An Imprint of HEADLINE PUBLISHING GROUP LIMITED

1

Disclaimer:

Cataloguing in Publication Data is available from the British Library

ISBN 978-1-03542-104-6

Compiled and written by: David Clayton
Editorial: Saneaah Muhammad and Matt Tomlinson
Designed and typset in Avenir by: Andy Jones
Project manager: Russell Porter
Production: Arlene Lestrade
Printed and bound in China

Headline's policy is to use papers that are natural, renewable and recyclable products and made from wood grown in well-managed forests and other controlled sources. The logging and manufacturing processes are expected to conform to the environmental regulations of the country of origin.

HEADLINE PUBLISHING GROUP LIMITED
An Hachette UK Company
Carmelite House, 50 Victoria Embankment, London EC4Y 0DZ

The authorised representative in the EEA is Hachette Ireland, 8 Castlecourt Centre, Dublin 15, D15 XTP3, Ireland (email: info@hbgi.ie)

www.headline.co.uk   www.hachette.co.uk

THE LITTLE BOOK OF

PATRICK MAHOMES

IN HIS OWN WORDS

UNOFFICIAL AND UNAUTHORIZED

CONTENTS

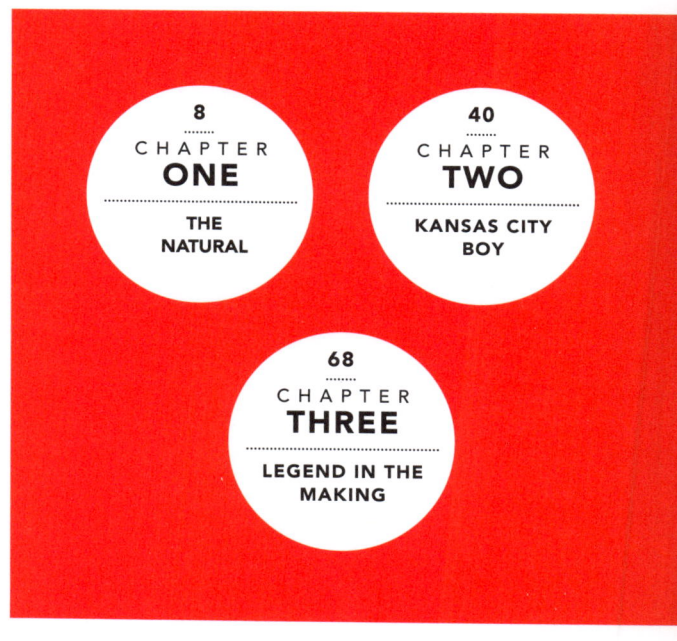

INTRODUCTION

Patrick Mahomes isn't just an athlete—he's a game-changer, a record-breaker, and the future of football. Born into a world of sports as the son of Major League Baseball pitcher Pat Mahomes, Patrick's destiny was set in motion from day one. While baseball was his first love and he was even drafted by the Detroit Tigers in 2014, Mahomes had other plans. He traded the diamond for the gridiron, choosing football at Texas Tech University. And boy, was it the right call.

With a rocket arm and a "gunslinger" style that defies logic, Mahomes started breaking records and wowing NFL scouts almost immediately. Capable of launching 80-yard bombs with pinpoint accuracy, he became the talk of the football world. Soon enough, The Kansas City Chiefs discovered his potential and brought him on board, seeing him as the heir apparent to veteran quarterback Alex Smith.

Fast-forward to today, and Patrick Mahomes has already cemented himself as one of the greatest quarterbacks in NFL history. With three Super Bowl rings (and counting), countless MVP awards, and a paycheck that places him alongside the highest-paid athletes in the world, Mahomes is rewriting the playbook on what it means to be a superstar. But beyond the jaw-dropping stats and mind-bending throws, he's also a devoted father, a philanthropist, and the kind of guy you want leading your team.

This small but mighty book is packed with the best quotes, jaw-dropping facts, and awe-inspiring moments from the life of Patrick Mahomes. Whether you're a die-hard Chiefs fan or just admire greatness, this is the perfect tribute to the man who's not just making history—he's shaping the future of football.

Chapter 1

The Natural

How Patrick Mahomes went from the talented son of an MLB pitcher to carving out his own legendary path in football, using the skills he mastered on the baseball field to craft a style of play that's entirely his own—and nothing short of brilliant.

The Natural

Baseball was everything to me.

Mahomes reveals his first love,
Esquire, October 2023.

> **"**
> Oh… I don't know.
> **"**

Talented at every pretty much every sport he competed in, this was Patrick's stock response to his mother's question of how he'd won his latest trophy! *Kansas City Star*, September 2018.

Stable, always there. Always there for us. Showed us you have to work hard to get what you want.

Describing his mother, kansascity.com, September 2018.

I just remember him being so excited to go to the yard every day. I'd have to hold him back just so I could get in the car before we left because he was ready to get out there. And he'd get there to the clubhouse, get his uniform on, and he'd be one of the first guys out on the field and, of course, I had to play catch and all that.

Pat Mahomes Snr.

Patrick's father recalls his son's early baseball obsession, nypost.com, February 2023.

The Natural

It's definitely the best I've felt all season. I've had to get control of my stuff this season. I've been working here and since before the season, getting my velocity up like it was today. I'm hard to hit.

High school baseball sensation Mahomes records 16 strikeouts as Wildcats beat Mount Pleasant 2–1, ETSN.fm, March 2014.

Baseball had been pretty much his whole life growing up, and he always played basketball, too. Those were his two sports. I was trying to keep him from playing football. But then his junior year in high school, he said he wanted to try this quarterback thing and see where it took him.

Pat Mahomes Snr.

Patrick's father tells *USA Today* about his son's sporting prowess, September 2018.

The Natural

Patrick was trying to figure out how I threw my fastball. He was talking to A-Rod (Alex Rodriguez) asking how he can hit the ball to right field like he did… he wanted to be part of the culture we had in our clubhouse.

LaTroy Hawkins

Mahomes' godfather recalls how a young Patrick had a thirst to learn, even as a child, GMTM.com.

The Facts #1

Growing up, Patrick's father, Pat Mahomes, nicknamed his son "Showtime" due to his athletic skill in so many different sports. He was also identified early on as possessing a photographic memory.

He thought he was Alex.

Randi Mahomes

Patrick's mother reveals her then five-year-old son's goal in life to be Texas Rangers baseball star Alex Rodriguez! Dailymail.co.uk, September 2024.

"

He learned how it works. How to gain those guys' respect, how to deflect credit. Walking the walk. That came at a very young age.

LaTroy Hawkins

Explaining how the youngster's sporting prowess in grade school helped make his school days more comfortable, kansascity.com, September 2018.

I knew he'd be a professional athlete when he was seven. I'm serious. There was never a question to him, and I knew he had the talent.

Randi Mahomes

Patrick's mother could see his potential from the get go... kansascity.com, September 2018.

"

I bet it feels amazing to be the quarterback who says, 'I'm going to Disney World' after winning the Super Bowl #Qbs.

"

A 17-year-old Mahomes on his personal Twitter (now X) account back in 2012—little did he know he'd be able to say it many times himself in years to come!

The Natural

The very first scrimmage that he played in fall in 2014. He had just gotten there in June. He threw five touchdown passes. He didn't know what he didn't know. Everybody was like, 'Holy cow, who is this?'

Kliff Kingsbury

Texas Tech coach recalls his first impression of an 18-year-old Mahomes, nytimes.com, January 2020.

I really think he's just scratching the surface (as a quarterback) with the time he played different sports throughout the year. When he really focuses on football the majority of the time I think you're really going to see him take off in that position.

Kliff Kingsbury

Texas Tech coach sees the potential in his new quarterback if he drops baseball! Foxsports.com, June 2014.

The Natural

I was a baseball player that just started playing football and he made me into this quarterback.

Mahomes pays homage to one of his biggest influences, Texas Tech coach Kliff Kingsbury, sports.yahoo.com, February 2019.

"

So much of what I do is because
I played baseball. I was a shortstop,
and out on the football field I'm
doing exactly what I was doing
as a shortstop. I'm hitting the first
baseman in the chest. All those
arm angles, throwing sidearm,
underhand, against the body all of
that is stuff I did as a shortstop.

"

The baseball-style quarterback reaping the
rewards of his multisport prowess, esquire.com,
October 2023.

Patrick is the poster child for the multi-sport athlete.

Adam Cook

Patrick's football coach at Whitehouse (Texas) High School on his star player's abilities, stack.com, January 2020.

Because he played multiple sports, the overlay of all of those experiences and skills are there in the NFL… It's all just one game for Patrick. It's always been just one big game, just on different playing surfaces. In high school football, you are guaranteed just 10 games. Instead [of only playing football], Patrick was always playing something and learning how to win along the way.

Adam Cook

More from coach Cook on how he believes Patrick developed into a superstar, stack.com, January 2020.

No more basketball. Basketball lasted all of one time.

"

Mahomes calls time on his basketball career, even if it never really got started! Esquire.com, October 2023.

Just his playmaking ability and the different arm angles and touch and incredible accuracy, it was phenom-type stuff. Even when the game seemed chaotic, it was never moving too fast for him. I had just never seen that before.

Kliff Kingsbury

Mahomes' Texas Tech coach on spotting Mahomes' early potential and uniqueness, *Time* magazine, October 2023.

The Natural

I think a lot of [my improvisation] is from baseball and how I could sling the ball across the diamond. I played shortstop my whole life. I never had my feet under me. I was always making throws across my body.

Mahomes reveals how he developed his football skills, *Texas Football* magazine, 2016.

"

One of my roommates from my freshman year, he came and sat beside me and was like, 'Dude, you've thrown the ball like 77 times for like 700 passing yards.' I was like, 'I did not even notice that. I was just out there throwing that thing.'

"

Mahomes' incredible stats against Oklahoma in October 2016—and the fact he was oblivious to it! Stack.com, October 2017.

Baseball, I felt like I almost already peaked. I felt like I knew everything about baseball. In football, I'm still learning something every single day.

Mahomes reveals why he didn't choose the baseball path—his thirst to learn and improve, kansascity.com, September 2018.

Ever since I was in high school, my parents left it all up to me and just said, 'Whatever you do, do the best you can and work as hard as you can.'

Looking back on his unpressurized path to playing football, "Pathway to the Pros", youtube.com, 2017.

I never worked out that was the biggest difference from going to college from high school where I was always playing football, baseball, and basketball so I never really had to work out.

On his limited workout time, "Pathway to the Pros", youtube.com, 2017.

'Every day is game day' means every day you have to bring it like you're at a game day, every single day in training, and that gets you where you want to be.

The early focus and determination of a future superstar, "Pathway to the Pros", youtube.com, 2017.

If I don't do everything the right
way in training, do it over again.
That really helped me out in college
becoming a next level quarterback,
not just a good quarterback.

More inspirational advice from Mahomes,
"Pathway to the Pros", youtube.com, 2017.

"

[I think it has to do] with just the fact that I've long-tossed since I was five years old. My dad, me and him, would always work on long-tossing back and forth. So me doing that all the time, it just built arm strength.

"

On where his arm strength developed from, "Pathway to the Pros", youtube.com, 2017.

The Natural

That is strictly from baseball.
To me, until I get those long tosses
in, I haven't loosened up my arm.
I haven't gotten my arm going.
It's the same as if someone runs
and loosens their legs. It's my
pattern.

On his practice of throwing the pigskin from
one endzone to the other to warm up—another
baseball-inspired trait. Stack.com, February 2021.

"

I think a big part of it was that playing quarterback felt creative to me. I loved that creativity, making things happen. I grew up watching Aaron Rodgers: he was my guy, and he kind of broke the mould of how to play quarterback, with the different arm angles and the way he extended the play. Playing like that really appealed to me.

"

On finding a way to make football more appealing than baseball, esquire.com, October 2023.

Chapter 2

Kansas City Boy

Patrick Mahomes had been catching the eye of the Texas Tech Red Raiders for some time, with scouts and coaches queuing up to watch this unique talent.

Now it was time to take the next step…

After talking with coach Kingsbury and my family, we feel this is the best decision for me moving forward.

Mahomes announcing his intentions to apply for early eligibility to enter the 2017 NFL Draft, NFL.com, January 2017.

The Facts #2

Kansas Chiefs drafted Texas Tech quarterback Patrick Mahomes after trading up to No. 10 in the NFL Draft. It had been 34 years since the Chiefs took a quarterback in the first round, namely Todd Blackledge in 1983.

Kansas City Boy

I want to win Super Bowls here… I want
to be great. I'll put that pressure on
myself, so we can do it, so it's not like
I feel any pressure from anyone else. I love
this game. I love working, so being able
to come in here every day is enjoying life.
People before you have built the
foundation, so you have to just go out
there and finish it off.'

Mahomes tells the Kansas press of his lofty
intentions, kansascity.com, September 2018.

He was meant to do this. You're going to see some stuff this year you've never seen before.

Pat Mahomes Snr.

Patrick's dad promises the Chiefs fans that they're in for something special after drafting his son, kansascity.com, September 2018.

Kansas City Boy

Everybody liked this guy. Couldn't find a guy who didn't like him… everybody fell in love with the kid and how he went about his business and how he played. That's not something that happens every year.

Andy Reid
Kansas City Chiefs coach on the immediate impact Mahomes had on everyone at Kansas, kansascity.com, April 2017.

" Right now Patrick isn't absolutely ready to play he's got some work to do. He's going into a great room… he can learn from Alex. We have to be patient with him. Tremendous upside. Good person, intelligent with great skill. "

Andy Reid

The coach welcomes Mahomes to Arrowhead, espn.com, May 2017.

You've got to learn from your mistakes. That gunslinger mentality to make the throws [is good], but when you have a defense like the Chiefs have, you have to make sure you protect the ball.

New Kansas City Chiefs recruit Mahomes admits he has to make adjustments to be the best he can be, kansascity.com, April 2017.

It's extremely exciting to play for a coach you know will coach you well. It's something you always want.

On the prospect of collaborating with coach Andy Reid, kansascity.com, April 2017.

That's pretty awesome. He's had a successful career in the NFL, so you know he's doing things the right way.

Rookie quarterback Mahomes looks to Chiefs veteran Alex Smith as a mentor in his early days at Arrowhead, kansascity.com, April 2017.

"

It's not like I mean to throw no-look passes… I think it kind of happens out of instinct.

"

Mahomes says one of his trademark moves comes from the gut, sportsillustrated.com, 2018.

We were in awe of what he was doing. We'd sit around talking about the throws he made on us in practice. We'd all talk about how he got us with this play or that play. When it came time for the Broncos game, we all had our popcorn ready. We were sitting there saying, 'Watch this,' or 'Look at this.'

We were starstruck when it came to the talent he had. There was no way he could throw the passes he could throw and not be successful. "

Derrick Johnson

Chiefs defensive team-mate recalls the day Mahomes was fully unleashed in the final game of the 2017 season against Denver Broncos, espn.com, September 2023.

The Facts #3

At 23 years old, Patrick Mahomes was announced as the 2018 MVP at the NFL Honors, after his first season as the Chiefs starting quarterback, making him the youngest recipient of the award since Dan Marino in 1984.

I get fired up seeing him live his dream and having his success just how much passion and heart he has.

Pat Mahomes Snr.

Patrick's father tells *USA Today* about his son's sporting prowess, September 2018.

Kansas City Boy

For a young guy, he's passed every test. They've been behind, and the game was on the line. He's made the plays for them to win. He's been able to get his team off to a quick start. He can make throws you don't even allow anybody to practice. The throws he makes, nobody can coach them but him.

James Harris

The NFL's first Black quarterback praises Mahomes, andscape.com, February 2019.

66

He doesn't seem like a guy who's going to get complacent and just enjoy what his success has been. I think he's a guy who's going to try to get better than he already is. If he gets any better than he is right now, I think the league is in for a helluva quarterback.

99

Doug Williams

The first Black quarterback to both start and win a Super Bowl predicts greatness, andscape.com, February 2019.

When you think about this league and the quarterbacks who are in this league, for a guy that young to have the season he's had and to be consistent. That's the key: He's not inconsistent at all. You're talking about a young guy who has picked up on this game probably quicker than anybody I've seen in this league… To do what he's done, it's incredible.

Doug Williams

The NFL legend on Mahomes' first Super Bowl MVP award, andscape.com, February 2019.

He's such an intelligent young man, with the intellect to be an NFL quarterback. I knew he could do this. He has always been so mature, so polite really, the All-American kid.

LaTroy Hawkins

Mahomes' godfather speaks highly of Patrick to *USA Today*, September 2018.

Kansas City Boy

When I entered the league, the big question about me was could I do the traditional stuff, could I stand in the pocket and make all the throws? I had to prove that I could do that. I had to win some trust.

On paying his dues and earning respect, esquire.com, October 2023.

For a kid to be in his first year as a starter and to do something only three guys have done throw 50 touchdown passes, throw for over 5,000 yards then lead his team to the AFC championship game, that's pretty amazing. Everybody was looking for him to have that rookie nosedive during the season it never happened. The kid just kept playing. He was consistent the whole year. The sky's the limit for him. He's special.

Warren Moon

NFL legend and fellow quarterback on Mahomes' bright future, andscape.com, February 2019.

The Facts #4

In 2019, "Mahomes Magic Crunch", a sugary frosted-flakes breakfast cereal, hit the shelves after a deal with midwestern supermarket chain Hy-Vee. Mahomes hoped to sell 50,000 of the exclusive cereal, with around 30% of profits going back to 15 and the Mahomes Foundation. The sales exceeded 300,000 units, earning the foundation $100,000.

"

All I know is that he's fun to watch.
He's must-see TV.

"

James Harris

The NFL's first Black quarterback and confirmed
Mahomes fan, andscape.com, February 2019.

The Facts #5

Patrick Mahomes was chosen as the cover star for EA Sports NFL game Madden for 2020 though there was a long-held (and partly true) belief that appearing on the Madden cover brought with it a curse for the following season. Would appearing on Madden 20 bring misfortune to Patrick?

It's pretty surreal to be on the
Madden cover and [the alleged
curse] is not a big deal at all.

Mahomes dismisses the hocus pocus surrounding
the Madden cover curse, mensjournal.com,
June 2019.

Kansas City Boy

There's only 30 or 31 people who have ever been on the [Madden] cover, all these legends of the game like Michael Vick, Antonio Brown and Tom Brady, so it's amazing feeling and bit surreal when I found out.

On learning he'd been selected as the cover for Madden 20, chiefswire.usatoday.com, April 2019.

He's a great quarterback, man.
He can run, throw, he can throw on
the run. He can make good reads.
A quarterback like that, it's really
hard to scheme for.

Xavier Rhodes

The Indianapolis Colts cornerback explains the
difficulties of facing Mahomes at the January 2020
Pro Bowl, skysports.com, August 2020.

Chapter 3

Legend in the Making

After his rookie season with the Chiefs, Patrick Mahomes became the first-choice quarterback, and some pretty special things begin to happen—and this precocious talent leads Kansas to a first Super Bowl success in 50 years…

The Facts #6

In February 2020, Patrick Mahomes was crowned Super Bowl LIV MVP—with 286 passing yards, three touchdowns (two passing and one rushing), and two interceptions—to become the youngest player ever to win the award, at 24 years and 138 days.

I think Tom [Brady] said it best—once you win that championship and you have those parades and you get those rings, you're not the champion anymore. You have to come back with that same mentality, and I learned from guys like that that have been the greatest of all time at the top of the level.

Mahomes' championship-winning mentality is relentless, washingtonpost.com, February 2024.

We never lost faith. That's the biggest thing. Everybody on this team, no one had their head down. We believed in each other. That's what we preached all year long.

Speaking after the Chiefs end their long wait to become Super Bowl champions after beating the 49ers, espn.com, February 2020.

"

We have heart. We never give up and those guys around us, the leaders on the team, have that mindset that we never give up.

"

More from Mahomes after beating the 49ers, espn.com, February 2020.

Legend in the Making

Man, at the end of the day, when you play against him your secondary has to step up. His arm is so talented that you can't zone it up or he's going to tear you apart.

Joe Haden
Pittsburgh Steelers cornerback on the impossible task of stopping Mahomes, skysports.com, August 2020.

The Facts #7

In July 2020, Patrick Mahomes reached an agreement with Kansas City Chiefs on a 10-year contract extension until the 2031 season. The deal was worth $503 million and was the largest contract in sports history, with Mahomes becoming the first athlete with a half-billion-dollar contract and the first NFL player to be the highest-paid athlete in the sports world.

And we're staying together…
for a long time. We're chasing
a dynasty.

Mahomes posts on his official X account after
penning a world record 10-year contract extension
with Kansas City Chiefs, July 2020.

66

This is a significant moment for our franchise and for the Chiefs Kingdom.

Clark Hunt

Kansas City Chiefs chair and CEO reflects on Mahomes' record deal, nfl.com, July 2020.

99

I can't say that the fifth-year [option] won't be an option or anything like that. It'd be hard for me to say that we'd have to use that. We feel that it is a priority when you have a great player, and when a great player is a priority, things get done.

Brett Veach

The Chiefs general manager on exercising the fifth-year option on Mahomes' contract, sportsillustrated.com, July 2020.

❝

Congrats to @PatrickMahomes on agreeing to terms on a 10-year extension worth $503 million. He gets $477M in guaranteed mechanisms and ability to have outs if guarantee mechanisms aren't exercised. No trade clause. First half billion dollar player in sports history. History made.

❞

Steinberg Sports

Official post on X from Mahomes' sports agency, July 6, 2020.

Legend in the Making

"

I'm honoured to become a part-owner of the Kansas City Royals. I love this city and the people of this great town. This opportunity allows me to deepen my roots in this community, which is something I'm excited to do.

"

In July 2020, with the ink barely dry on his half-billion dollar contract, Mahomes announced he was investing in local MLB side Kanas City Royals, businessinsider.com, February 2024.

They beat us good. The best I've been beaten in a long time.

Reflecting with brutal honesty on the 31–9 loss to the Buccaneers at Super Bowl LV—arguably the first major setback of his stellar career start, sportsillustrated.com, February 2021.

My dad lost in the World Series and still continued to battle and be himself. Obviously, it hurts right now, but we will get better. We can't let this define us.

Mahomes showed an attitude and maturity beyond his years after being outperformed by Tom Brady of the Buccaneers at Super Bowl LV in 2021, cnn.com, February 2023.

I've seen how people, on Twitter, have tweeted and said, 'Oh, you're not full Black.' But I've always just had the confidence and believed in who I am. And I've known that I'm Black. And I'm proud to be Black. And I'm proud to have a white mom too. I'm just proud of who I am. And I've always had that confidence in myself. The more I mature, I've learned that I was blessed to be in the situation that I was in.

Mahomes discusses his mixed race heritage, and the trolls, in a revealing interview, gq.com, July 2020.

The Facts #8

In August 2021, Patrick Mahomes was named the best player in the NFL by his peers in NFL Network's annual countdown of the league's top 100 players. It was Mahomes' first win in "The Top 100 Players" list, having finishing fourth twice (in 2019 and 2020).

66

I kind of get back to that backyard-style football a little bit too much. And you could definitely see that in the Super Bowl. I mean, there were times that pockets were clean, and I was still scrambling.

99

Reflections on the Super Bowl loss to the Tampa Bay Buccaneers and where he could improve his game, theringer.com, August 2021.

Legend in the Making

I look at every game pretty much the same.
I go through the whole entire season,
we go through the whole entire scheme
evaluation, and we just figure out what we
did good and what we did bad. And I mean,
we did a lot of good last year, I think we get
lost in that with how we played in the Super
Bowl. And so we take from that and try to
learn ways to get better and try to find a
way to win at this next year.

More reflections on the Super Bowl loss
to the Buccaneers and learning from setbacks,
theringer.com, August 2021.

"

He's a nice guy. We all know that. He's a good kid… But down in there [in the heat of battle], he's gritty and he wants to get after you every opportunity he has. Most of all, he wants to be great and everyone around him to be great. He has the ability at that position to do that, and he's not afraid to be coached.

"

Andy Reid

Coach praises Mahomes' humility and willingness to continue learning and improving, andscape.com, January 2022.

Legend in the Making

He's not afraid to study hard. He's not afraid to work out hard, go the extra mile with diet, strength training, all those things, flexibility. He goes and tries to do it the best he possibly can. And as a result, you get what you got there. What we've seen—we've been spoiled with for the last few years—[is] he's a pretty spectacular player and we're lucky to have him right here in Kansas City.

Andy Reid

More praise for Mahomes' attitude and work ethic, andscape.com, January 2022.

The Facts #9

During Kansas City's playoff win against the Pittsburgh Steelers in January 2022, Mahomes's stats read 404 passing yards, five touchdown passes, 29 yards rushing and an interception, making franchise history, and ousting his former mentor Alex Smith for the single game passing yards record.

Legend in the Making

Everyone has got a thought about Patrick Mahomes. This guy is so gifted, and he can make so many plays for ya in so many different ways. With Mahomes, what's so unusual is that he… he can just do everything. He can get out of the pocket and make a play, and he's shown he can throw on the run and make things happen. He also does it from the pocket. He's just a gifted guy.

Joe Gibbs

Former Washington Redskins coach and Hall of Famer Joe marvels at Mahomes' repertoire, *Rise of the Black Quarterback* by Jason Reid, August 2022.

The Facts #10

Patrick Mahomes won his second NFL MVP award for the 2022 season. After winning in 2018, he was again voted as the NFL's best by his fellow professionals. During the 2022 season, Mahomes threw for a career-high 5,250 yards and led the NFL with 41 touchdown passes. He has thrown 4,000 or more yards in each of the five seasons since he became the Chiefs starting quarterback.

Legend in the Making

Just trying to give them a blueprint of how the week goes. Obviously, you can see it on the schedule, but I want them to see it from a player's perspective.

Mahomes speaks about trying to guide newer players through the Super Bowl LVII clash with the Philadelphia Eagles, cnn.com, February 2023.

"

The Super Bowl week is special, it's a special week, but it's not about being down there for the week of the Super Bowl, it's about winning the game. I want guys to keep that at the front of their mind. Enjoy the whole entire week but make sure you're prepared to go out there and play your best football as well.

"

More thoughts from Mahomes ahead of the Super Bowl LVII clash with the Philadelphia Eagles, cnn.com, February 2023.

The Facts #11

Patrick Mahomes capped an incredible run as Kansas City Chiefs defeated Philadelphia Eagles 38–35 in the Super Bowl LVII: It gave Mahomes his second league championships and a second NFL MVP award, becoming the first player in the history of the NFL to win multiple league championships and MVPs in his first six seasons.

"

It felt great until I kind of rolled it a little bit. I thought I felt really good and then that happened, and I had a lot of soreness going through into halftime and was able to move it around, kind of get taped up a little bit and go out there in that second half. It didn't feel good, but I was going to leave it all out there.

"

Mahomes aggravated a high ankle sprain in the first quarter of the Super Bowl win over Philadelphia Eagles but refused to come off injured and stayed on to help his team win, espn.com, February 2023.

Legend in the Making

The failures... they give you a greater, greater appreciation to be standing here as a champion.

Mahomes reflects that his second Super Bowl win was all the sweeter for suffering defeat at the same stage in 2021, espn.com, February 2023.

"

My baby boy did what he always do. You know he's gonna show up and show out, and I'm just glad he did it.

"

Pat Mahomes Snr.

Mahomes' proud father reacts after his son's match-winning performance against the Eagles, cnn.com, February 2023.

Chapter 4

Family, Friends, and Faith

A snapshot of the people Patrick Mahomes loves the most, and words from those who love him most—plus his beliefs, inspirations, habits, and hobbies!

You're not going to find a more superstitious guy, so when it's freezing and snowing in December in Kansas City, you're still going to see him wearing those shorts at Patrick's football games.

LaTroy Hawkins

Patrick's godfather on Pat Snr.'s superstitious traits watching his son, usatoday.com, September 2018.

"

It hasn't [changed]. They treat me exactly the same as when I was a little kid. They still talk trash, still kinda rip at me a bit, but at the same time, we like to just go out, play *Call of Duty* and talk about each other's lives at the same time.

"

On the importance of being grounded by his childhood buddies, yahoosports.com, February 2019.

My girlfriend, she gets mad at me sometimes when you start playing *Call of Duty*, and then you look down and it's, like, three hours from when you started. I might get a knock at the door in the game room that says I need to stop playing, but I usually get a couple matches in after that.

On his gaming habits, yahoosports.com, February 2019.

66

My Christian faith plays a role in everything that I do. I always ask God to lead me in the right direction.

99

On receiving advice from a higher power, chvnradio.com, February 2023.

I know that I am here for a reason, to glorify Him. It means everything, not only about my football career but all the decisions that I've made.

The Chiefs quarterback reveals his faith, outkick.com, February 2023.

"

I have a faith backing, and I know why I am here. It's not about winning football games. It's about glorifying Him.

On his true purpose, outkick.com, February 2023.

Nick Kyrgios: Pleasure bro…
   let's play some pickleball soon."
Patrick Mahomes: Yessir!
   I gotta get some pickleball
   going, bro.

Australian tennis star Kyrgios' and Mahomes'
exchange at Wimbledon over Instagram, July 2024.

66

They do a lot for me. So I'm gonna take care of them as well.

99

Mahomes' generous Christmas 2023 gift to each of his Chiefs offensive line team mates was an electric golf cart, customized with their name and number! Chiefswire.usatoday.com, December 2023.

I was like the best friend, in the friendzone forever. I used to walk her to class and was trying to flirt. When I was a sophomore in high school, and she was a junior, I actually got her a rose and I was kinda, like, I had a crush on her. But I was giving the rose as a joke, but kind of a quotation 'joke'.

Mahomes on courting future wife Brittany, gq.com, August 2023.

 I thought it was the sweetest thing. **"**

Brittany Mahomes

Patrick's wife on receiving THAT rose, gq.com, August 2023.

[It's] gotta be the cell phone. On social media, I'll throw a few jokes here and there. I try to stay tuned in to the fans and my friends and family and everything like that, man, I see everything.

One of Mahomes' answers on GQ's "10 Things Patrick Mahomes Can't Live Without", youtube.com, September 2023.

Greatness, dawg. Greatness.

Mahomes in awe after watching Dallas Mavericks star Kyrie Irving's incredible buzzer beater, which gave Dallas a 107–105 victory over the Denver Nuggets, sportsillustrated.com, March 2024.

Family, Friends, and Heroes

I have to keep my body in shape, so no one tell my trainer this or the Chiefs, but I'm a big snacker. I like to eat a lot of chips, candy, whatever it is, especially at nighttime, which I know is the worst part of the day to eat snacks. I always grab a purple bag of Doritos which I just got on.

I used to be a Cool Ranch guy but
now I'm on the purple bag, or
I grab some gummies with like the
Jolly Rancher gummies.

"

Mahomes's snacking secrets revealed on GQ's
"10 Things Patrick Mahomes Can't Live Without",
youtube.com, September 2023.

Family, Friends, and Heroes

66

She's never not working. Even when she's taking her downtime, she's working on something. Shooting a music video or singing a song or writing a song. You can see it by how she talks. Even when she's talking about football, when she's learning it, you can see her business mind putting it together. It's almost like she's trying to become a coach. 'Why can't you try this, this, and this?' She's asking the right questions.

99

On friend and fellow superstar Taylor Swift, *Time* magazine, April 2024.

"

I've been a fan of ketchup for as long as I can remember.

Mahomes' 2018 confession led to a sponsorship deal with Hunt's Ketchup, businessinsider.com, February 2024.

Family, Friends, and Heroes

He has a tattoo artist literally in the room. I'm like, 'Dude, you do not actually have to get a tattoo of our autographs.'

99

Mahomes explains how US musician Post Malone ended up with tattoos of Patrick and Travis Kelce's signatures inscribed on his body as a forfeit for multiple beer pong defeats, gq.com, 2020.

> A lot of what I've become was being in the locker room and seeing professional athletes and how hard they work, how they have to strive to be great every single day. I'm hoping I can make those memories for my kids. Obviously, they're still young. Being able to have them at the Super Bowl and hopefully win it and be down in that confetti, it's something that hopefully they'll be able to remember for a long time.

On the importance of having his family share the historic moments, kansascity.com, February 2024.

Family, Friends, and Heroes

This week is awesome for them because they get to come, basically we call it vacation. So they get to go on a vacation. We were hoping for a little warmer weather. I'm sorry Vegas, coming from Kansas City, minus 30°F, I thought we were going to get like 70°F out here.

Mahomes bemoans the unseasonably cool Las Vegas weather ahead of Super Bowl LVIII for his wife and kids, kansascity.com, February 2024.

"

He can go to a Luke Combs concert with cowboy boots on and drink beer, or he can go to a Drake concert and have the most fun and enjoy himself that way. There's nothing but his genuine, authentic self. And I think that's a beautiful thing.

"

Kliff Kingsbury

Former Texas Tech coach pays an affectionate tribute to his former protégé, time.com, April 2024.

I definitely have the dad bod a little bit. I'll also say I have a great body for a quarterback. You've got to have some padding in there to take the hits that we take.

Poking fun at his own physique, but he accepts it gives him the necessary tools to do his job more effectively! Time.com, April 2024.

"
She wants to hold him, and take care of him, and everything like that. She wants to play all day, and we have to tell her to be gentle. And we have to tell her to don't throw him like a toy baby. That's a real baby you got there.

"

On the birth of his first son, Patrick "Bronze" Lavon Mahomes III, and how daughter Sterling was adjusting to her baby brother, SportsRadio 610, December 2022.

Family, Friends, and Faith

I'm a little disappointed I'm going to miss Christmas Eve with my kids, and Christmas morning and miss Santa coming.

Super Bowl on the horizon or not, Mahomes would prefer to spend Christmas with his wife and kids, Pro Football Talk, December 2023.

"

I think both my parents just really taught me how to follow my dreams. They didn't care if I was an athlete, they didn't care where I was going, they just told me to follow my dreams, do whatever I could to have no regrets at the end of the day. And so I think that's what I'm trying to do with my kids now—obviously I'm trying to parent in my own way, but I want them to enjoy life.

"

On his parenting style, sheknows.com, February 2024.

Family, Friends, and Faith

Everybody sees the game days.
They don't see the day-to-day grind.
They don't see how you have to
manage playing football and being
a dad and being a husband.

On the grit behind the NFL glitz, *Quarterback*
docuseries, Netflix, July 2023.

"

It's football. You're gonna have highs; you're gonna have the lows. You put so much into this that you want to win, you want to succeed. And you want to win that Super Bowl at the end of the year. But I have to be a dad too. I have to be a husband.

"

On achieving a work-life balance, *Quarterback* docuseries, Netflix, July 2023.

When my kids grow up, I want them to see that dad wasn't just gone just to be gone. I was gone doing something, to build, to be great. So, whenever they get older, they can see how hard I worked.

On ensuring his kids understand his sacrifices were for them, *CBS Mornings*, July 2023.

"

I think now, being able to go home and see my daughter and see my son, I have a better understanding of being present and enjoying it.

"

On enjoying the here and now with his young family, *CBS Mornings*, July 2023.

To my wife, Brittany, my baby girl, Sterling, and my son, Bronze, this crazy life that we are living means nothing without you.

The doting husband and father pays tribute to those he loves the most during his 2023 NFL Honors MVP award acceptance speech, independent.co.uk, July 2024.

"

Y'all gotta back up. We are not pros.

"

Mahomes warns the crowd, as he and Travis Kelce take on Stephen Curry and Klay Thompson in The Match charity golf challenge, aol.com, June 2023.

The Facts #12

15 and the Mahomies is a charitable foundation dedicated to improving the lives of children. The Foundation supports initiatives that focus on health, wellness, communities in need of resources, and other charitable causes and was established by Patrick Mahomes in 2019.

We are excited and proud to support Special Olympics Missouri in its mission to promote the power and joy of sports through outstanding athletes.

Mahomes speaks of his foundation's support for the Special Olympics Missouri (SOMO), which received a grant through the 15 and the Mahomies Foundation's signature program, 15 for 15. The program supports 15 youth charitable initiatives that focus on academics, science, the arts, classroom supplies, athletics, children with disabilities, after-school programs, and more.

I work on it. I think that's something that gets lost in this. Look at how he brought the three-pointer into what it is today. He's made such an impact on the game. It changed the entire sports world. I think that's something I'm going to try to continue to do in the NFL.

Mahomes cites Stephen Curry's impact in basketball as his inspiration to do something similar in football, time.com, April 2024.

You see the creativity they had.
They played at such a high level,
but they enjoyed it when they did.
That's a lot of what you see
from me.

"

Mahomes pays respect to the Black quarterbacks
who inspired him, upi.com, February 2023.

The Negro League Museum is a special place. The history you learn there is [why] I would recommend everyone go. My dad talked to me about Satchel Paige my entire life.

On the importance of Black history, upi.com, February 2023.

To be in this moment, on this stage, and to be able to show where we have come as a league, will be just the start of it. We want to make sure we set the stage for generations to come.

On being a role model to other Black athletes, upi.com, February 2023.

He understands how he's a pioneer in the sense that he's paving the way for a lot of a lot of young football players and definitely a lot of young Black football players.
I think it's really cool that we get to experience this with him.

Travis Kelce

Mahomes' teammate and close friend is enjoying the journey Mahomes is on, upi.com, February 2023.

66

Just like #ChiefsKingdom has always been there for me and my family, we want to be there for them.

99

Mahomes takes to X after the Kansas victory parade shooting, February 2024.

Family, Friends, and Faith

Playing high school basketball also had a huge influence on the way I play. I was a point guard, and in many ways that's exactly how I feel now. I'm still the point guard, trying to get the ball to people in space, get the ball to them in a position to score. In a lot of ways, it's exactly the same thing.

The point guard quarterback credits yet another sport for his unique style, esquire.com, October 2023.

> **"**
> It is what it is, dog. Who doesn't love some good locker-room banter, man? Shoutout to Ja'Marr Chase for holding it down for his QB, but don't you ever disrespect Pat Mahomes now. If you want to talk your s**t, talk your s**t, pimp. Just better back it up.
> **"**

Travis Kelce

Responding to an opponent's trash talk about buddy Pat Mahomes and calling out Ja'Marr Chase, who hinted he didn't know who Mahomes was, nfl.com, June 2023.

Burrowhead my ass, it's Mahomes' house.

Travis Kelce
Responds to the Cincinnati mayor Aftab Pureval's trash talk ahead of AFC championship game in January 2023. Bengals quarterback Joe Burrow held a 3–0 record against Mahomes going into the game and referred to the Chiefs' Arrowhead Stadium as 'Burrowhead'. A fired-up Chiefs team won this encounter 23–20, biography.com, 2023.

"

Travis is definitely the best player I've thrown to. With how big he is and the way he is able to run routes and make plays happen, is a really rare thing.

"

The mutual respect between Mahomes and Kelce is clear, NBC's Pro Football Talk, January 2024.

Travis has always been Travis. He's been himself the whole time. He's still Travis Kelce. He'll still walk through the stadium and treat everyone like they're his best friend and he's always going to be like that. It hasn't been any different to me.

Teammate and close friend Mahomes on how Travis' increased stardom has not changed him one iota, NBC's *Pro Football Talk*, January 2024.

"

Travis is definitely my closest teammate. I would say our friendship is more like a brotherhood—we're brothers now and our families get along together. I'm part of his family and he's part of mine.

"

Brotherly love—Chiefs style!
NBC's *Pro Football Talk*, January 2024.

Chapter 5

Super Bowls and Super Stats

The upwards trajectory of Patrick Mahomes shows no signs of stopping anytime soon. Here are some of his stellar moments, reflections, and observations of why the kid from Texas is something pretty special…

The Facts #13

Patrick Mahomes made the 200th touchdown pass of his career, reaching the milestone in his 84th game (against the New York Jets in October 2023), to break Dan Marino's NFL record. Marino threw his 200th TD pass in his 89th NFL game with Miami in 1989.

He also surpassed 25,000 yards the previous week against Chicago, accomplishing accomplished the feat in 83 games, seven faster than Matthew Stafford's record.

First off, this is a great environment, man. It really is. But we did hear it all week about playing a road game, and we're here to prove a point and show that we can play anywhere.

Mahomes shares his thoughts with CBS reporter Tracy Wolfson on the field following his first career playoff road win (27–24) over the Buffalo Bills, January 2024.

I love being at Arrowhead. I love being at Arrowhead and playing in front of that crowd. But when you're on the road, it's you versus them. It's you versus everybody in the stadium, and you have to come together as a team and let guys do that.

You saw that in the game today.
I went over to the defense, and
I told them. I said, 'Y'all shut it down,
and we'll win this football game.
We'll go to the AFC Championship
Game.' And they did.

"

More from Mahomes after beating the Bills,
nfl.com, January 2024.

The Facts #14

Moments after leading a winning scoring drive in overtime, Patrick Mahomes was named Super Bowl LVIII MVP for the third time after beating the San Francisco 49ers 25–22 in Las Vegas, equalling Joe Montana and moving closer to Tom Brady's record five.

"

You be you all day!

Travis Kelce

Inspiring words to best buddy Patrick Mahomes ahead of Super Bowl 2024, talksport.com, March 2024.

He's one of the best coaches of all time; I believe he is the best coach of all time.

Mahomes pays tribute to Chiefs coach Andy Reid, cbsnews.com, February 2024.

For me, he brings out the best in me because he lets me be me. He doesn't try to make me anyone else, I don't think I would be the quarterback that I am if I didn't have coach Reid being my head coach.

More praise for Chiefs coach Andy Reid, inc.com, February 2024.

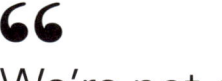

We're not done.

Mahomes tells CBS there is much more to come with the Chiefs after he personally posts 333 yards, two touchdowns, and 66 rushing yards on his way to Super Bowl MVP honours for a third time, sportsillustrated.com, February 2024.

"

We've got a young team; we're going to keep this thing going.

"

On continuing the Chiefs' Super Bowl successes, usatoday.com, February 2024.

Super Bowls and Super Stats

I think it puts the team in a different echelon. We understand how hard it is to do that in this league, with all the parity that's in this league. Whenever you play 20 games and have a ton of success and then have to rebuild again that next year—because once you win the championship, that year's over. You have to rebuild and go for it again.

Already looking ahead to the next success, usatoday.com, February 2024.

"

I mean, I'm gonna celebrate tonight. I'm gonna celebrate at the parade. And then I'm gonna do whatever I can to be back in this game next year and try to go for that three-peat.

"

History three-peating itself? Mahomes looking to maintain the Chiefs' NFL dominance for as long as possible, usatoday.com, February 2024.

Super Bowls and Super Stats

Our mindset was: Go win the game right here. Once we got that ball—we fell short in regulation; we're not going to do that again. We're going to go out there and win the game.

Relfections on his third Super Bowl win with the Chiefs, espn.com, February 2024.

Let's go win this thing.

"

Chiefs quarterback Mahomes enters the
huddle ahead of overtime in the Super Bowl LVIII
against the 49ers to issue a simple mandate!
Espn.com, February 2024.

Super Bowls and Super Stats

It's culture, man. I got brought into this culture. Alex Smith was leading the team. They had the pieces in place and Coach Reid has been the ultimate leader and I got brought in and I just trying to exemplify that, and he keeps pushing to be even better.

Mahomes—the ultimate collaborator—shares the glory after a third Super Bowl success, espn.com, February 2024.

"

He brings out the best in me because he lets me be me. I think that's important. He's not trying to make me anyone else. I don't think I'm the quarterback that I am if I didn't have Coach Reid as my coach. He wants you to be the best person you can be.

"

Mahomes pays homage to his mentor, Coach Reid, after beating the 49ers in Las Vegas, espn.com, February 2024.

Super Bowls and Super Stats

I've lost the Super Bowl, and I know how bad that hurts. You want to make sure you stay away from that feeling. So I think even more than hoisting that trophy, when you lose and you're in that locker room and you feel like you were that close and you didn't get it, I'm gonna look more even to stay away from that feeling than I am hoisting the trophy.

On how avoiding the pain of defeat can act as inspiration, nytimes.com, February 2024.

66

That's the goal: You want to play as long as they'll let you play. It takes a lot of work outside of the building. It takes taking care of your body. It takes eating healthy and (trying) to get rid of the dad bod that I got. But try to do whatever you can just to get healthy and go out there and be the best player that you can be.

99

On his playing career lasting another 15 years, nytimes.com, February 2024.

Okay, let's see how much fun we can have.

Mahomes sums up his attitude to football and life in general, esquire.com, October 2023.

"

I'm trying to enjoy those moments because I know it doesn't last forever, even though we want it to.

"

A philosophical Mahomes looks at the brevity of a sporting career at the very top, and ensuring he absorbs the moment, *CBS Mornings*, July 2023.

It's the start of one. We're not done.

Following the Chiefs' third Super Bowl win in five years, Mahomes responds to CBS reporter Tracy Wolfson after she asks, "Is it a dynasty now?" *CBS Sports*, February 2024.

> **I'm going to Disneyland!**

After winning his third Super Bowl MVP award following the Chiefs' 25–22 overtime win against the San Francisco 49ers, Mahomes follows in the tradition started years before of telling the cameras he was headed for his third trip to the happiest place on earth, nbc.com, February 2024.

Super Bowls and Super Stats

> [Coach] Andy Reid always reminds us that there are no dead routes. Patrick has such great vision. He sees everything, sometimes before it happens, so you always have to be ready. He will throw it to anybody, anywhere, at any time. And it will be on the money.

Justin Watson

The Chiefs receiver waxes lyrical about his teammate, theatlantic.com, February 2024.

 This is a business trip!

Mahomes speaks ahead of the Super Bowl
LVIII versus the 49ers, nbcsports.com,
February 2024.

Chapter 6

The GOAT Debate

Patrick Mahomes is, in many people's eyes, the greatest NFL player of all time. Mahomes plays this down, but others are more effusive.

Here are a selection of thoughts, theories, and opinions from a selection of voices, including the man himself—and the man long considered the GOAT...

I mean, what a great young player. So impressed with his poise, his leadership. He is spectacular.

Tom Brady

NFL legend Brady recognises the ability of the (potential) future heir to his crown, nbcsports.com, January 2019.

> **Patrick Mahomes might become the GOAT...**

Jack "CouRage" Dunlop

The popular YouTuber and gamer shares his thoughts with his sizeable social media following on X, February 2024.

The GOAT Debate

There are so many guys, they were at such a high level for such a long time. In order to be in that conversation, you have to do that on a year-to-year basis. You can't take it for granted that you did it the year before.

Mahomes downplays the GOAT debate and says he has plenty more to achieve before he's part of that discussion, nbcsports.com, April 2024.

Every week, Patrick Mahomes does a bunch of things that shouldn't be possible for a human.

Computer Cowboy

An NFL account puts Mahomes' superhuman exploits eloquently into perspective in an X post, December 2018.

Notable NFL Records

(as at August 1, 2024)

Consecutive 300-plus passing yard games:
8 (tied)

Total yards (passing and rushing) in a season:
5,608 (2022)

FASTEST TO:

10,000 career passing yards: 34 games
25,000 career passing yards: 83 games
100 career passing touchdowns: 40 games
200 career passing touchdowns: 84 games

IN A PLAYERS FIRST 50 GAMES:
Passing yards: 15,348
Passing touchdowns: 125

IN A POSTSEASON:
Passing touchdowns: 11 (2021) (tied)
Total touchdowns (passing and rushing):
12 (2019, 2021)

Kansas City Chiefs Records

(as at August 1, 2024)

Touchdown passes in a game: 6 (2018, tied)

Touchdown passes in a season: 50 (2018)

Passing yards in a season: 5,250 (2022)

Passing yards in a playoff game: 404
(2021–22 playoffs)

Attempts in a game: 68 (2022)

Completions in a game: 43 (2022)

Career rushing touchdowns by a
quarterback: 12

Career rushing yards by a quarterback: 1,936

Career completions: 2,386

The GOAT Debate

He enjoys the moment. You know it's not the truth, but he plays the game like it doesn't mean anything. He just lets it go. He's himself in those moments. That's what you want from a quarterback.

Joe Montana

NFL legend and former quarterback on what makes Mahomes great, time.com, April 2024.

He's as much a quarterback as he is an artist, expanding our vision for what football can be. That's what I thought when he made that scramble in overtime last night. The play was inevitable, and also baroque. It was genius.

Jayson Buford

GQ sportswriter Jayson Buford eloquently describes why he believes Mahomes to be the GOAT following his third Super Bowl win, gq.com, February 2024.

I think when I'm looking at guys in pro football, quarterbacks, Patrick's the one that really stands out and has [done] so. They've done a great job since he's really taken over.

Tom Brady

The NFL legend responding to the question as to who will be his successor at the top of the tree, sportsillustrated.com, October 2023.

NFL Awards

(as at August 1, 2024)

3× Super Bowl champion (LIV, LVII, LVIII)

3× Super Bowl MVP (LIV, LVII, LVIII)

2× NFL Most Valuable Player (2018, 2022)

NFL Offensive Player of the Year (2018)

2× First-team All-Pro (2018, 2022)

Second-team All-Pro (2020)

6× Pro Bowl (2018–2023)

2× NFL passing touchdowns leader
(2018, 2022)

NFL passing yards leader (2022)

Bert Bell Award (2018)

He's seen the greats. He strives
to be the greatest. Without saying
anything, that's the way he works.
He wants to be the greatest
player ever. That's what he wants
to be.

Andy Reid

The Chiefs head coach on Mahomes' ambition and
drive, theringer.com, February 2023.

I've had the privilege of coaching a lot of incredible athletes and special people in my career, and Patrick is without question on that list of players. The best part is he's still early in his career. He's a natural leader and always grinding, whether that's on the field, in the weight room or watching film, he wants to be the best. He's a competitor and his teammates feed off his energy. He makes us all better as an organization and we are blessed he's going to be our quarterback for years to come.

Andy Reid
Singing Mahomes' praises, nfl.com, July 2020.

The GOAT Debate

I'm not even close to halfway, so I haven't put a lot of thought into it. I mean, your goal is to be the best player that you can be. I know I'm blessed to be around a lot of great players around me.

Mahomes responds to the question of whether he can emulate Tom Brady's seven Super Bowl wins ahead of the game with San Francisco 49ers, nytimes.com, February 2024.

"

Right now, it's doing whatever I can to beat a great 49ers team and try to get that third ring. And then if you ask me that question in 15 years, and I'll see if I can get close to seven. But seven seems like a long way away still.

"

Mahomes tells reporters to ask him in 2039 about catching Tom Brady's seven Super Bowl wins, nytimes.com, February 2024.

It's hard to describe someone that good. He's a legend. He's a blessing.

Brett Veach
Chiefs general manager reacts after Mahomes' superb display in the 17–10 AFC Championship Game to book a place in the Super Bowl against the 49ers, kc05.com, January 2024.

Pat is clearly the biggest name in football right now. For him to still be in his 20s and not slowing down anytime soon means he's also the future of football.

Travis Kelce

The Chiefs team mate on the "future of football", time.com, April 2024.

I guess at this point, I take it for granted, but I know we're in every single game I've ever played in with him, no matter what the score is, no matter how much time is left.

Travis Kelce

Chiefs tight end on knowing his team are never beaten while Mahomes is on the field, espn.com, February 2024.

"

It really is cool. Doing it at Arrowhead... it's a tremendous honor to be a part of this organization and be able to do stuff like that at this stadium. It'll be stuff I remember the rest of my life.

"

Mahomes on becoming the fastest NFL quarterback to reach 25,000 passing yards following a 41–10 win over the Chicago Bears, arrowhead.com, September 2023.

You have to build a consistency of a career. You see that in any sport. I've had a great run. I think I've done a great job so far.

Mahomes on maintaining his standards, time.com, April 2024.

"

That's something I'll talk about when I'm done playing. Then people can make those decisions.

"

Another response by Mahomes to the GOAT debate, time.com, April 2024.

"

I've had at least one of the top three starts to a career, I'll put it that way.

"

Mahomes' response when asked where he felt he stood in the GOAT discussion… Tom Brady won his third Super Bowl MVP when he was 37 years old. Joe Montana was 33. Mahomes is just 28. Time.com, April 2024.